Chicago Writer™ Books

A Guide for

Young

Chicago

Writers

From Brainstorm to Bestseller—
Get Your Ideas Into Words and
Your Words Into Print

Acknowledgements

iWrite Publications Inc. gratefully acknowledges all of the publishers who took the time to verify their information and complete our questionnaire. It is their efforts that make this guide valuable to the writers and editors who wish to do business with them.

Chicago Writer

Keep up-to-date with resources and issues that affect writers, editors, and publishing professionals. Visit our web site at http://www.ChicagoWriter.com.

Published by:
❚Write Publications Inc.
PO Box 10923, Chicago, IL 60610-0923
USA

ISBN 13: 978-1-933048-39-0

Contents

Introduction

This guide was written to assist young writers to prepare professional-quality articles and manuscripts and to get these works noticed by magazine editors and book publishers.

Using the Guide

Use the magazine and book publisher summaries in this guide to research a publisher's releases. The publishers' sites provide more in-depth profiles of the companies, as well as information such as: job opportunities, writer's guidelines, current publishing lists, and additional contact information.

Before approaching a publisher, remember two things:
- do your research and
- query first.

You'll get a much better response for your efforts.

Corrections/Updates

As diligent as we might be, businesses change. If you find any information that is out-of-date or publishers that you think should be added or removed from the guide, please drop us an email at iwriteinc@aol.com to let us know. We appreciate your assistance.

You can view a list of corrections and updates to this book at http://www.chicagowriter.com/errata.htm.

Good luck in your writing quests!

Writing Output

If my doctor told me I had only six months to live,
I wouldn't brood. I'd type a little faster.
—Isaac Asimov

Nine out of ten writers, I am sure, could write more.
I think they should and, if they did, they would find
their work improving even beyond their own,
their agent's, and their editor's highest hopes.
—John Creasey

Two thousand words a day is very good going.
—Evelyn Waugh

Writing Your Stories

Writers get inspiration from almost anywhere and anything. Just as your ideas are uniquely yours, so is your writing process. Although it is helpful to learn how successful writers write, you won't succeed until you find your own special process and your own unique voice.

One way to learn what works best for your writing is to look at one topic or subject from different angles: facts, feelings, investigation, and imagination.

Here are some techniques to help you get started.

Just the Facts

Factual writing is most like journalistic writing with the who, what, where, when, and why of the story taking center stage.

It is the style a writer uses to describe events or observations—what happened at the concert; how the school's new dress code will be implemented; where to find the most popular jeans at the best deals.

The writing is factual and precise. The writer doesn't make guesses or interject opinion.

> Try this» Describe something that happened to you in the last two days. Include who, what, where, when, and why. Keep it to about three paragraphs. Write it in the first person (e.g., "I saw" or "I heard") or third person (e.g., "The car stopped" or "The music blared"). Keep it concise and factual.

Feelings

Writing about feelings and emotions puts the human factor into your human interest stories. Evoking feelings draws the reader into the story and makes him care about your characters.

The best way to incorporate feelings into your work is to describe the actions or reactions of the characters to reflect the emotion you want to convey.

For instance, rather than say, "I was scared," it is better to write, "My stomach fell and my palms began to sweat when the car stopped unexpectedly on the darkest part of the road."

When you evoke feeling rather than state it, you allow your reader to feel what you are writing about. They participate in your story.

> Try this›› Take the story you wrote from the last exercise and add feelings and emotions. Describe both the internal and external reactions of everyone in your story.

Investigation

Investigative writing uses interviews or research techniques to teach the reader something. It's the type of writing you do when your teacher assigns a term paper or a research report. It includes quotes and citations of sources.

This is the style of writing used in the academic and scholarly fields. An investigative story can include history, statistics, geographic origins, first person experience, and current news items.

The writing is factual and provides a context to better understand an idea or concept.

> Try this›› Take one aspect of the story you wrote from the first exercise and investigate it. Write a few paragraphs about this concept that will help your reader better understand your initial story. For example, if you wrote your first story about a car accident you witnessed, investigate the safety record of one of the cars involved or the accident experience at the site of the crash. If you wrote your first story about waiting in line for concert tickets, investigate how online brokers have changed the way people buy tickets or the growth in the type of music you were going to see.

Imagination

This writing is pure dreaming. It is what science fiction, fantasy, and paranormal fiction is made of. It doesn't have to make sense. It doesn't have to have any basis in reality. It is the most creative type of writing.

> Try this›› Rewrite the first story you wrote in an imaginative way. Create scenes that couldn't possible occur on Earth. Make it whimsical or make it wild. Go nuts!

Pulling It All Together

Some of the best writing incorporates some of all of the previous techniques.

If you're writing nonfiction, accuracy of your facts are most important, but you also want to present your information in a creative fashion that will interest your readers.

If you're writing fiction, your creativity and the flow of your story are most important, but you also want to know enough about your characters and their world to keep the story credible and your readers hooked.

One last assignment:

> Try this» Write a new story or article incorporating the techniques you've learned. Test to determine what combination works best for the subject matter or type of story you're writing.

Other Tips to Improve Your Writing

- Read! The more you read, the more good writing you'll be exposed to.
- Try other genres. If you write nonfiction, try poetry. If you write fantasy, try historical fiction. Stretch your imagination and you'll stretch your talent.
- Take a class. Learning something new is a great way to grow and become a more interesting person and a more interesting writer.
- Study how other writers write. Read a biography of your favorite writer. If you hear of writers speaking at a local book store or library, go and ask them a question about how they write.
- Volunteer. Write for your favorite cause. Not-for-profit organizations are always looking for help to spread their missions.
- Keep writing. The more you write, the better you'll become.

Writers and Writing

There is only one trait that marks the writer.
He is always watching. It's a kind of trick of mind
and he is born with it.
—Morley Callaghan

A great writer creates a world of his own
and his readers are proud to live in it.
—Cyril Connolly

We romantic writers are there
to make people feel and not think.
—Barbara Cartland

Refining Your Work

Fact of a writer's life is that most good writing comes from rewriting. Before you send your work to an editor or publisher—or release it to the public in any way—make sure that it's your best effort.

Beginning writers tend to err on the side of using too many words rather than too few. Make every word count. Have a thesaurus and dictionary handy when you are writing. Select the best words to express your ideas. Eliminate the unnecessary ones.

Editing your own work is very difficult to do. Because you created the article or story, your mind tends to read what you meant to say or wanted to convey rather than the actual words on the page. Here are some tips for refining your work on two levels: content editing and copy editing.

Content Editing

Content editing focuses on the information in your story. Is the work conveying your ideas accurately? Can anyone who reads your story understand what you're trying to say? Ask yourself:

- Is there a defined beginning, middle, and end to my article?
- Are the facts in my story correct?
- If I've quoted someone, is the quote accurate? Is the source's name spelled correctly?
- Is my characters' dialogue believable?
- Is each idea clearly defined?
- Does each paragraph, section, or chapter flow into the next?
- Am I using the simplest words possible to express my meaning?
- Am I using as few words as possible?

Content editing is important in fiction when you are using facts that you want your readers to believe to carry your story along. If you use an actual location, person, or event, it's important to get it right. A classic example of getting it wrong occurred a few years ago on the television show *ER*. To showcase the Chicago location, the writer had two of the main characters *rendezvous* at the corner of Clark and Dearborn. The next day, no one in Chicago remembered anything that happened during that episode. They were all talking about the fact that that writer didn't know—or check—that Clark and Dearborn streets run parallel to each other and never intersect. Content mistakes like that throw your readers out of your story rather than keeping them involved.

Content editing is critical in nonfiction. Publishers of nonfiction have a legal obligation to be sure that the facts they present in the books and articles they publish are as accurate as possible. If you are writing nonfiction, check and recheck all of the information in your story before you submit it for sale and retain your notes and research sources.

Copy Editing

Copy editing focuses on spelling, grammar, punctuation, and usage. It is extremely difficult to proofread your own work. You know what you're trying to say and so that's what your brain reads—even if words and punctuation are missing! Here are a few tips to make proofreading easier:

- Print out your pages. Online editing is difficult even for experienced editors. Things always look different on paper. You might want to print the pages double spaced. It will give you more room to note changes and corrections. Use a colored ink like red or green to mark your changes. They will stand out better when you're typing the edits into your manuscript.

- Don't trust your spell checking software exclusively. Just because a word is spelled correctly does not necessarily make it the correct word. For instance, "I herd that you were looking for some one to write a book about hoarse shows." That went through me spell check just fine. Get it? Mistakes are going to get into print. It happens, but they get into print more often when you don't proofread carefully.

- Try reading each line backwards. You'll be more apt to notice incorrect wording if it's not in context. Try reading the pages upside down. You'll be amazed at what pops out at you.

- Set aside time for editing/proofreading separate from writing. For instance, if you write late at night, do your proofreading in the morning. Distance your editorial self from your creative flow.

- Get someone else to look at your manuscript. Even an untrained eye is going to notice mistakes when reading something fresh.

Some great copy editing resources to have are:
- A good dictionary
- Roget's (or an alphabetical) thesaurus
- *The Chicago Manual of Style*
- *Fowler's Modern English Usage*
- *The Elements of Style* by Strunk and White

Approaching Publishers

Unless you have a relative in the publishing business or you've decided to self publish your book or magazine articles, you will need to know how to approach a publisher to sell your work.

The most important thing to know when approaching magazines or book publishers is that most of the people submitting work are adults—that's your competition. The next most important thing to know is the reasons most work is rejected: it's been submitted to the wrong publisher or it's not what the author claimed or promised it would be.

The best ways to avoid these pitfalls are:

- Do your homework. Submit your work only to those editors whose periodicals or companies publish the type of work that you write.
- Be honest. Don't tell an editor that you have an article about cutting edge design in sports cars when what you've written is an essay about your opinion of the latest Ford Mustang.
- Submit only your best work. In spite of the fact that you will probably be making many revisions before the article is published, never submit sloppy work expecting the editor to catch the typos.
- Be professional. This is the publishing major leagues. Act as though you belong.

Magazine Submissions

Magazine editors need freelance writers almost as much as writers need the opportunities. Most magazines these days work on very tight budgets and no longer have the money to have a fulltime writing staff to produce every issue. Freelance writers fill the gap because editors only have to pay them when they write something the editors can use.

Most editors like to see samples of someone's writing before they assign an article. In the business, this is known as "clips." Clips are copies of published articles. They are not printouts of stuff you have on your computer. You can create a portfolio of clips two ways. First, many magazines will send a writer a clip of the published article when the magazine goes to print. It is generally a reprint of the page or pages of the magazine containing the article. If a magazine doesn't send a clip, purchase a copy of magazine that contains your article, carefully cut out the full pages, and make copies. Retain the originals in your portfolio and always send copies out for review (you most likely will not get them returned).

Once you have a number of clips to your credit, you can enclose one or two with every query letter to show the editor your past work. Until then, it is best to write the article you want to sell before you propose it to the editor and enclose the completed article with your query letter. You most likely will be asked to make revisions to it before it is published, but the editor can clearly see what type of writing to expect from you.

1. **Select your target magazine.**
   Write for a magazine that you routinely read or use this guide to select a magazine that publishes articles on the topics about which you wish to write. Once you select the magazine you'd like to write for, study the periodical's submissions guidelines. Pay attention to their submission requirements.

2. **Begin your query letter with a brief summary of the article.**
   Include what it's about and the length (e.g., 2,000 words). Describe your unique slant on the topic and list the resources or experts you intend to use in writing your story.

3. **Add a paragraph describing any writing experience you have.**
   You want to explain why you are the best person to write the story without exaggerating or being arrogant.

4. **Give the editor your contact information.**
   Provide an address, phone, and email contact. Make it as easy as possible for the editor to do business with you.

5. **Thank the editor for his or her time and close.**
   Sign the letter. Enclose some clips or your sample article as well as a self-address, stamped envelope for a reply.

Only submit one article idea to an editor at a time. You will appear more focused and professional. And only submit your article or idea to one editor at a time. There are no multiple submissions in magazine work. Magazines are only looking for something that no one else has.

Book Proposals

The first step in the publishing process is to submit a book proposal to a publisher.

1. **Select your target publishers.**
   Use this guide or some other publishing resource to research the organizations that publish the type of books that you write. Go to that publisher's web site to verify current contact information and locate any submission guidelines they might have.

Follow their guidelines. Believe them if they say they don't want self-help books. Believe them if they say no electronic queries. You have to work with the system here, not try to change it. Don't give the publisher a reason to reject your idea before you even submit it.

It is standard industry practice to submit proposals to one publisher at a time, give them a time window (usually four to six weeks) for a response, then move to the next on your list. If you want to cut down the wait time, submit your proposal to two or three publishers at one time, but be sure to indicate on your cover letter that it is a simultaneous submission. You do not need to inform each publisher to whom you have also submitted, but you do need to let them know that other publishers are considering the proposal at the same time. Research the publisher and direct your proposal to the editor you think is most appropriate to receive your submission. No "To Whom It May Concern" submissions. No phone queries. And no electronic submissions unless the publisher specifically states they are acceptable.

2. **Begin your letter with a brief introduction including the title of your book and a short description of it.**
Briefly introduce yourself, the title of your book, and a short description of the contents. This should be about fifty or fewer words. Think of what the blurb on the back cover of your book would contain. You want to hook the editor by describing the unique idea or angle your book is taking.

3. **Indicate your target audience.**
You need to tell the editor who would be interested in buying your book and why. If you don't know who will buy your book, the publisher is not going to figure it out for you.

4. **What else on the market is similar to your book? What is on the market that your book will complement?** You are competing for the editor's attention against hundreds of manuscript submissions each year. If you can position your book in the marketplace and explain to the editor how your book is different, superior, more complete, has a broader reach, or deeper focus, you've done much of the work the editor needs to prepare to sell the book to the publisher. This puts you head and shoulders above the crowd.

5. **Indicate why you selected this publisher for your submission.**
Let the editor know that you researched their publishing house by listing related titles or indicating how your book would enhance their publication range.

6. **Add a brief closing.**
   Thank the editor for his or her time and close. Again, briefly include preferred contact information for yourself and include a self-addressed, stamped envelope for a response. (If you want the publisher to return your entire package, be sure to enclose a large envelope with enough postage.)

7. **The second part of the submission includes the table of contents and a sample chapter or two (not the first chapter).**
   Text pages should always be printed out in a simple font (Times Roman or Courier), double-spaced with one-inch margins all around. This is the easiest format to read—and editors read a lot of manuscripts. Also put a header on each page with the book's title, your last name, and a page number.

   Unless an electronic submission is requested by the editor, do not send the material on disk. If the editor has requested electronic submission, follow her specifications or if not provided, format the material as PDFs (portable document format). There is more chance of compatibility and less chance of transmitting a virus.

Put all of the materials in a large envelope so that the pages do not need to be folded. Remember, if you want any of your material returned to you, include a large self-addressed, stamped envelope in the package as well. Address the package to the specific editor and send first class mail.

A Note on Follow-up Calls

It is perfectly acceptable to phone the editor after a week or so to make sure he has received your materials. This is also a good time to ask about the editor's response timeframes and to reiterate that your submission is a simultaneous submission, if applicable. Be friendly, don't push.

One contact call and a second follow-up call if the editor has not responded in the allotted time are acceptable, and that's it. Further calls most probably will not help your case. If an editor has not or cannot make a decision on your book, it's fair to move on to the next publisher on your list and submit your proposal to them.

Submission Tracking Form

Track your article submission activity. Indicate whether the editor passed on or purchased your submission. Also, did you receive a subsequent assignment from the editor because of your submission?

Date	Title **Editorial Contact**	Pass	Sold	Assign
5/1/2007	"Gearing Up for Summer Sports" Jane Fort / Editor in Chief *Teen Magazine* Pub Date: _____ Payment $_____	☐	☐	☐
	  Pub Date: _____ Payment $_____	☐	☐	☐
	  Pub Date: _____ Payment $_____	☐	☐	☐
	  Pub Date: _____ Payment $_____	☐	☐	☐
	  Pub Date: _____ Payment $_____	☐	☐	☐
	  Pub Date: _____ Payment $_____	☐	☐	☐
	  Pub Date: _____ Payment $_____	☐	☐	☐
	  Pub Date: _____ Payment $_____	☐	☐	☐
	  Pub Date: _____ Payment $_____	☐	☐	☐

Date	Title **Editorial Contact**	Pass	Sold	Assign
	Pub Date: _____ Payment $_____	☐	☐	☐
	Pub Date: _____ Payment $_____	☐	☐	☐
	Pub Date: _____ Payment $_____	☐	☐	☐
	Pub Date: _____ Payment $_____	☐	☐	☐
	Pub Date: _____ Payment $_____	☐	☐	☐
	Pub Date: _____ Payment $_____	☐	☐	☐
	Pub Date: _____ Payment $_____	☐	☐	☐
	Pub Date: _____ Payment $_____	☐	☐	☐
	Pub Date: _____ Payment $_____	☐	☐	☐
	Pub Date: _____ Payment $_____	☐	☐	☐

Advice to Young Writers

It is not wise to violate the rules
until you know how to observe them.
—T.S. Eliot

Writing has laws of perspective, of light and shade,
just as painting does, or music. If you are born knowing
them, fine. If not, learn them.
Then rearrange the rules to suit yourself.
—Truman Capote

Nothing you write, if you hope to be any good,
will over come out as you first hoped.
—Lillian Hellman

Talking About Your Writing

Never talk about what you are going to do
until after you do it.
—Mario Puzo

Don't tell anybody what you book is about and
don't show it until it's finished. It's not that anybody
will steal your idea, but that all that energy that goes into
the writing of your story will be dissipated.
—David Wallechinsky

You lose it if you talk about it.
—Ernest Hemingway

If the poem can be improved by its author's explanations,
it never should have been published.
—Archibald MacLeish

Working With Your Editor

Congratulations! You got "The Call." After weeks or months of waiting through the submissions process, an editor has phoned you to say he is interested in buying your article or publishing your book. Time to celebrate. You've gotten over a hurdle that many adult writers never do—you're about to become a published writer.

Now, hold onto your hat. The real work begins.

Rule Number One when working with editors is: The editor is your boss. No matter how great, fabulous, or unique your article or manuscript is, you're not going to see it in print unless you get it past the editor. Be respectful and listen to what they have to say. Then do what you've agreed to do.

Rule Number Two: Everyone makes revisions. No article or manuscript is published "as is" from the author. Stephen King, J.K. Rowling, and Nora Roberts all make changes recommended by their editors. Regardless of how good a writer you are, the editor has the inside track on what is best for her magazine or what types of books sell best in his line.

Magazine Articles

When and editor contacts you about purchasing your article or assigning you a story, you most likely will be asked to sign a contract. What you are signing over are your copy rights to the article. Three types of rights are most common:

First North American Serial Rights: This means that the magazine is buying exclusive rights to be the first serial (magazine) publishers of your article in North America. Once you sign this away, you cannot sell the same article to anyone else until the magazine issue is published and on the news stands.

Electronic Rights: This means that the magazine is buying exclusive rights to publish your article in any electronic means it wishes. Once you sign this away, you cannot even post the article on your personal website or page. Only the magazine can publish the article electronically.

All Rights: Many magazines request that all rights be signed over to them. Once you sign all rights away, the magazine owns your article forever.

If you have any questions or concerns about the rights that the magazine is requesting, it is best to contact an entertainment or intellectual property attorney for advice.

Once the contract is signed, you editor will then let you know what changes he wants in the article, what slant he wants on the assigned story, and when the final product is due.

Your editor is always there to answer your questions and assist when possible, but most magazine editors are so busy that the successful magazine writer will be the one who is most self sufficient and can meet deadlines as agreed.

Book Contracts

Once the editor informs you that the publishing house is interested in your manuscript, she will either mail or fax to you the company's standard publishing contract. No matter how excited you are about getting published, don't sign anything until you have the contract reviewed by an attorney working for you.

Find an entertainment or intellectual property attorney to read over the contract and explain all of its facets to you. Publishing is a specialized industry with terminology and standards all its own. The initial draft of the contract coming from the publisher is very highly weighted in favor of the publisher. Your attorney is the person who will look after your interests. Of course, if you have made the sale through a literary agent, the agent will take care of the contractual details.

Once the contract is signed, you will probably meet in person or by phone with your editor to go over suggested revisions and the publishing time lines, as well as other important items like how royalty payments will be made.

Talk to your editor as both a boss and a trusted advisor. Ask questions and tell her of any concerns that you have. Listen to her feedback and understand that what she's telling you is coming from years of experience. (Even if your editor is new to the game, she works for someone who has lots more experience.) Then, get to work and get your book out.

Chicago YA Book Publishers

The following section contains summaries of Chicago-area book publishers that release titles for the young adult market.

Before you send a query letter, visit the publisher's web site and check:

- Genres of titles they publish
- Submission guidelines
- Changes in editorial contact information

Submit only your best work and be professional!

Academy Chicago Publishers

363 West Erie Street, Chicago, IL 60610
(312) 751 7300

What They Publish

Publishes fiction and nonfiction.

Currently accepting new manuscripts on all topics.

Representative Titles/Articles
- *The Children of Dickens*
- *The Children's Shakespeare*
- *Four Classic Ghostly Tales*

How to Get Connected

Contact:
Dr. Anita Miller, President and Editor
Jordan Miller, Vice President

Accepts queries by: ☐ Email ☐ Fax ☐ Phone ☒ Letter
See submission guidelines online.

Email: academy363@aol.com
Web Site: http://www.academychicago.com

African American Images

1909 West 95th Street, Chicago, IL 60643
(773) 445 0322

What They Publish

Publishes Africentric books on self-esteem, collective values, liberation, and skill development.

Currently accepting new manuscripts on all topics. Query first.

Representative Titles/Articles
- *Grandma's Ashanti Cloth*
- *Hip Hop Land*
-

How to Get Connected

Contact:
Jawanza Kunjufu, President

Accepts queries by: ☐ Email ☐ Fax   ☐ Phone ☒ Letter
See submission guidelines online.

Email: aai@africanamericanimages.com
Web Site: http://africanamericanimages.com

Chicago Review Press

814 North Franklin Street, Chicago, IL 60610
(312) 337 0747

What They Publish

Publishes nonfiction topics under three imprints:
- Chicago Review Press: general nonfiction and a growing line of children's' activity books.
- A Cappella Books: nonfiction, primarily on music.
- Lawrence Hill Books: progressive political and Black interest.

Representative Titles/Articles
- *American Revolution for Kids*
- *When Race Becomes Real*
- *Snake Hips*

How to Get Connected

Contact:

Linda Matthews, Publisher
Cynthia Sherry, Acquisitions Editor, Chicago Review Press imprint manuscript queries

Accepts queries by: ☐ Email ☐ Fax ☐ Phone ☒ Letter
Send query with outline and sample chapter. Must include an SASE.
Do not send fiction, computer disks, or self-help manuscripts.

Email: csherry@ipgbook.com or
mailto:edit@ipgbook.compublish@ipgbook.com (for queries)
Web Site: http://www.ipgbook.com

Cricket Books

An Imprint of Carus Publishing
PO Box 300, Peru IL 61354

What They Publish

Publishes children's books for all ages.

Representative Titles/Articles

- *Double Dare to Be Scared*
- *Chief Sunrise*
- *Pigs Can Fly*

How to Get Connected

Contact:
John Allen, Editor

Accepts queries by: ☐ Email ☐ Fax ☐ Phone ☒ Letter
Query first. See submission guidelines online.

Email:
Web Site: http://www.cricketmag.com

Crossway Books

Division of Good News Publishers
1300 Crescent Street, Wheaton, IL 60187
(630) 682 4300

What They Publish

Publishes religious books from a conservative, evangelical Protestant point of view; fiction; and children's books with a Christian viewpoint.

Representative Titles/Articles

-
-
-

How to Get Connected

Contact:

Marvin Padgett, Vice President, Editorial

Accepts queries by: ☐ Email ☐ Fax ☐ Phone ☒ Letter
Send query letter or manuscript. Must include an SASE. Do not phone or send ideas for picture books. Replies in 8–12 weeks.

Email:
Web Site: http://www.crosswaybooks.com

Kazi Publications, Inc.

3023 West Belmont Avenue, Chicago, IL 60618
(773) 267 7001

What They Publish

Publishes nonfiction and fiction about Islam, Islamic culture and civilization, and the Middle East for children and adults.

Representative Titles/Articles

- *What Everyone Should Know About Islam and Muslims*
- *Ideals and Realities in Islam*
- *Sufi Women of America: Angels in the Making*

How to Get Connected

Contact:
Mary Bakhitiar

Accepts queries by: ☐ Email ☐ Fax ☐ Phone ☒ Letter
See submission guidelines online.

Email: info@kazi.org
Web Site: http://www.kazi.org

Medallion Press, Inc.

212 Franklin Street, Suite 2, Barrington, IL 60010
(847) 756 4316

What They Publish

Publishes paperback fiction for young adults.

Representative Titles/Articles

- *Secrets*
- *Horse Passages*
- *Stones of Abraxas*

How to Get Connected

Contact:

Pam Ficarella, Editor in Chief
Peggy McMillan, Acquisitions Editor

Accepts queries by: ☐ Email ☐ Fax ☐ Phone ☒ Letter
Submission guidelines on website. Responds if interested.

Email: pam@medallionpress.com
Web Site: http://www.medallionpress.com

Moody Publishers

820 North LaSalle Street, Chicago, IL 60610
(312) 329 2102

What They Publish

Publishes Christian literature for an evangelical Christian market of young people and adults.

Representative Titles/Articles
- *The Love Language of God*
- *Unlocking the Bible Story*
- *A Place of Quiet Rest*

How to Get Connected

Contact:

Greg Thornton, Vice President, Executive Editor

Accepts queries by:　☐ Email　☐ Fax　☐ Phone　☒ Letter
Send proposal with one or two sample chapters or a synopsis that describes the proposed work's theme and target audience. Do not phone, show up without an appointment, submit inappropriate ideas, or send complete manuscripts. Include return postage if you want your submission returned. Responds in 8 weeks.

Email: pressinfo@moody.edu
Web Site: http://www.moodypublishers.com

Polychrome Publishing Corporation

4509 North Francisco Avenue, Chicago, IL 60625
(773) 478 4455

What They Publish

Publishes multicultural fiction and nonfiction (with an emphasis on Asian American themes) for children; some nonfiction directed at parents as teaching aids.

Representative Titles/Articles

- *Striking It Rich*
- *Children of Asian America*
- *Almond Cookies & Dragon Well Tea*

How to Get Connected

Contact:

Sandra Yamate

Accepts queries by: ☐ Email ☐ Fax ☐ Phone ☒ Letter
Send query letter and/or complete manuscript. Stories and plots must have authenticity with the cultures they describe. Do not send fables, folk tales, or animated animal stories. Replies within 6–8 months.

Email: polypub@earthlink.net
Web Site: http://www.polychromebooks.com

Third World Press

PO Box 19730, Chicago, IL 60619
(773) 651 0700

What They Publish

Publishes books by and about African Americans; children's fiction and nonfiction; preschool readers, picture books, vocational books; fiction and nonfiction—primarily politics, cultural history, philosophy, and poetry for African American adults and children.

Currently looking for biographical, spiritual, educational, political, and health-related works.

Representative Titles/Articles

- *I Look at Me*
- *The Story of Kwanzaa*
- *The Sweetest Berry on the Bush*

How to Get Connected

Contact:

Gwendolyn Mitchell, Editor

Accepts queries by: ☐ Email ☐ Fax ☐ Phone ☒ Letter
Accepts unsolicited work in January and July. Responds in 8–10 weeks.

Email: twpress3@aol.com
Web Site: http://www.thirdworldpressinc.com

Urban Research Press

840 East 87th Street, Chicago, IL 60619
(773) 994 7200

What They Publish

Publishes biographies of well-known African Americans and Jazz musicians; books about real estate, finance and social studies; and children's books.

Representative Titles/Articles

- *Autobiography of Black Jazz*
- *The American Story in Red, White, and Blue*
- *Norman Granz: The White Moses of Black Jazz*

How to Get Connected

Contact:

Dempsey J. Travis, Publisher

Accepts queries by: ☐ Email ☐ Fax ☐ Phone ☒ Letter
See submission guidelines online. Query only. Do not send complete manuscript.

Email: travisdt88@aol.com
Web Site: http://www.urbanresearchpress.com

Albert Whitman and Company

6340 Oakton Street, Morton Grove, IL 60053
(847) 581 0033

What They Publish

Publishes fiction, nonfiction, and language arts for children.

Representative Titles/Articles
- *Fox and Fluff*
- *Wanda's Monster*
- *Birthday Zoo*

How to Get Connected

Contact:
Kathleen Tucker, Editor-in-Chief

Accepts queries by: ☐ Email ☐ Fax ☐ Phone ☒ Letter
Send for writer's guidelines with SASE. Study previous Albert Whitman books before submitting a manuscript. Do not phone. Responds in 12–16 weeks.

Email:
Web Site: http://www.awhitmanco.com

What makes a good writer of history is a guy who is suspicious. Suspicion marks the real difference between the man who wants to write honest history and the one who'd rather write a good story.
—Jim Bishop

The thriller is an extension of the fairy tale.
It is melodrama so embellished as to create the illusion that the story being told, however unlikely, could be true.
—Eric Ambler

The mystery story is really two stories in one: the story of what happened and the story of what appeared to happen.
—Mary Roberts Rinehart

A good science fiction story is a story with a human problem, and a human solution, which would not have happened without its science content.
—Theodore Sturgeon

YA Book Clubs

Most often book clubs purchase the rights to publish/sell books from other publishers. For instance, a book club might purchase the rights to publish a Harry Potter novel from the original publisher, Arthur Levine Books. It would then create its own cover and binding and then offer the book to its club members at a discount from hardcover retail price.

However, book clubs also purchase manuscripts directly from authors as well. Especially if the book is well written and covers a genre or topic that the club thinks would appeal to its members and cannot find on the already published market.

As with any other publisher:
- query first,
- only send your best work, and
- be professional.

Arrow Book Club

577 Broadway, New York, NY 10012
(212) 343 4469

What They Publish

Publishes fiction and nonfiction for grades 4–6.

Representative Titles
- *The Nutshell Library*
- *Back to the Divide*
- *Gatekeepers #2: Evil Star*

How to Get Connected

Contact:
Jean Feiwell, Publisher

Accepts queries by: ☐ Email ☐ Fax ☐ Phone ☒ Letter

Email:
Web Site: http://www.scholastic.com

Junior Library Guild

80 Broad Street, Suite 3002, New York, NY 10004
(212) 233 6874

What They Publish

Publishes fiction and nonfiction for preschool through high school readers.

Representative Titles

- *A Swift Pure Cry*
- *Rucker Park Setup*
- *Resurrection Man*

How to Get Connected

Contact:

Susan Marston, Editorial Director

Accepts queries by: ☒ Email ☐ Fax ☐ Phone ☒ Letter

Email: editorial@juniorlibraryguild.com
Web Site: http://www.juniorlibraryguild.com

Kids Book Planet

15 East 26th Street, New York, NY 10010
(212) 651 7351

What They Publish

Publishes fiction and nonfiction for ages 6–12.

Representative Titles
- *Hoot*
- *Maniac Magee*
- *Gandhi*

How to Get Connected

Contact:
Kaylee Davis, Editor in Chief

Accepts queries by: ☐ Email ☐ Fax ☐ Phone ☒ Letter

Email:
Web Site: http://www.bookplanetbookclub.com

Lucky Book Club

577 Broadway, New York, NY 10012
(212) 389 3077

What They Publish

Publishes fiction and nonfiction for grades 2–3.

Representative Titles

- *Can It Rain Cats and Dogs?*
- *Zen Shorts*
- *Jigsaw Jones*

How to Get Connected

Contact:
Tamar Mays, Senior Editor

Accepts queries by: ☐ Email ☐ Fax ☐ Phone ☒ Letter

Email:
Web Site: http://www.scholastic.com

Teen Age Book Club

577 Broadway, New York, NY 10012
(212) 343 4528

What They Publish

Publishes fiction and nonfiction for grades 7–12.

Representative Titles
- *The Amber Spyglass*
- *The Subtle Knife*
- *The Will of the Empress*

How to Get Connected

Contact:
Greg Holch, Senior Editor

Accepts queries by: ☐ Email ☐ Fax ☐ Phone ☒ Letter

Email:
Web Site: http://www.scholastic.com

Magazines for YA Markets

The magazines included in this section are from all across the country. Since it is rare that magazine editors would want to meet with a writer in person, it is not necessary to be the same geographic location to do business with them.

Many of these magazines only accept work from young writers and that gives you an added edge in getting your work accepted.

Before submitting a query or work to a magazine, review the magazine's web site, understand the submission guidelines, and know what types of writing the editors look for by reviewing several issues of the periodical. (Check past articles in their online archives or at your area library.)

- Be sure that your article or story is what the editor asked for.
- Make sure it is your best effort.
- Be professional.

Breakaway Magazine

8605 Explorer Drive, Colorado Springs, CO 80920
(719) 531 3400

What They Publish

Publishes articles on extreme sports, Christian music artists, and new technology relevant to teenaged boys.

Looking for personal experience articles; adventure, humor, and suspense stories.

Representative Articles
- When Nature Attacks
- Dream Surf Camp Who's Who
- Fathers, Flying and Faith

How to Get Connected

Contact:
Michael Ross, Editor
Jeremy Jones, Associate Editor

Accepts articles by: ☒ Email ☐ Fax ☐ Phone ☒ Letter

Email: –

Web Site: http://www.breakawaymag.com

The Concord Review

730 Boston Post Road, Suite 24, Sudbury, MA 01776
(800) 331 5007

What They Publish

Publishes academic work by secondary students of history from around the world.

Looking for essays 4,000–6,000 words long.

Representative Articles
- Greek Enlightenment
- Journey to the West
- British Rule in Egypt

How to Get Connected

Contact:
Will Fitzhugh, Editor

Accepts articles by: ☐ Email ☐ Fax ☐ Phone ☒ Letter
See submission guidelines online.

Email: Fitzhugh@tcr.org

Web Site: http://www.tcr.org

CosmoGirl

The Hearst Corporation
224 West 57th Street, 3rd Floor, New York, NY 10018
(212) 649 3851

What They Publish

Monthly magazine for teen girls 11–17.

Looking for first-person stories, relationship stores, and personal experience articles.

Representative Articles
- Kelly Confidential
- Guy Dilemma
- The Rich Girls' Workout

How to Get Connected

Contact:
Susan Schulz, Editor in Chief

Accepts articles by: ☒ Email ☐ Fax   ☐ Phone ☒ Letter
See submission guidelines online.

Email: inbox@cosmogirl.com

Web Site: http://www.cosmogirl.com

Guideposts Sweet 16

1050 Broadway, Suite 6, Chesterton, IN 46304

What They Publish

Bimonthly magazine for teen girls 11–17.

Looking for true stories—your real-life dramas and everyday experiences.

Representative Articles
- The Big Cover-Up
- Boy Crazy
- Everyday Angel

How to Get Connected

Contact:
Editor

Accepts articles by: ☒ Email ☐ Fax   ☐ Phone ☒ Letter
See submission guidelines online.

Email: writers@sweet16mag.com

Web Site: http://www.sweet16mag.com

Gumbo Teen Magazine

Strive Media Institute
1818 North Martin Luther King Drive, Milwaukee, WI 53212
(414) 374 3511

What They Publish

Magazine for teens by teens.

Looking for articles of all types. All articles are written by teens. No adult may write for this magazine.

Representative Articles
- Summer Movie Spectacular
- The Price of Style
- How to Over Achieve, Not Stress Out

How to Get Connected

Contact:
Keenya Hoffmaier, Editor
Tiffany Wynn, Managing Editor

Accepts articles by: ☒ Email ☐ Fax ☐ Phone ☒ Letter
See submission guidelines online.

Email: info@mygumbo.com

Web Site: http://www.mygumbo.com

I Love Cats

16 Meadow Hill Lane, Armonk, NY 10504

What They Publish

Publishes general interest cat stories for the entire family.

Looking for feature stories about cats and their owners, (no talking cats, please), interesting or odd happenings with cats, tips for cat owners, health issues, nonfiction pieces, behavior problems, that sort of thing. Please do not send stories about cats that go or live outdoors.

Representative Articles
- The Cat Who Stole Christmas
-

How to Get Connected

Contact:
Lisa Allmendinger, Editor

Accepts articles by: ☒ Email ☐ Fax ☐ Phone ☒ Letter
See submission guidelines online.

Email: ilovecatseditor@sbcglobal.net

Web Site: http://www.iluvcats.com

Insight

55 West Oak Ridge Drive, Hagerstown, MD 21740-7390
(301) 393 4038

What They Publish

Publishes stories for teens 13–19.

Looking for true stories, profiles of Christian celebrities, profiles of outstanding Seventh-day Adventist youth, and general articles.

Representative Articles
- For the Cause
- Fire in the Attic
- Battle Scars

How to Get Connected

Contact:
Dwain Esmond, Editor
Michelle Bergmann, Associate Editor

Accepts articles by: ☒ Email ☐ Fax ☐ Phone ☒ Letter
See submission guidelines online.

Email: insight@rhpa.org

Web Site: http://www.insightmagazine.org

Listen Magazine

The Health Connection
55 West Oak Ridge Drive, Hagerstown, MD 21740
(301) 393 4010

What They Publish

Magazine for teens promoting tobacco, drug, and alcohol prevention.

Looking for true life stories with a "tell me something I don't already know" angle.

Representative Articles
- Raimi Merritt: Wakeboard Champion
- 25 Things to Try Before Trying Drugs
- Geocaching

How to Get Connected

Contact:
Celeste Perrino-Walker, Editor

Accepts articles by: ☒ Email ☐ Fax ☐ Phone ☒ Letter
See submission guidelines online.

Email: editor@listenmagazine.org

Web Site: http://www.listenmagazine.org

Merlyn's Pen

PO Box 2550, Providence, RI 02906
(401) 751 3766

What They Publish

Online magazine that publishes fiction, essays, and poems by teens. Also provides resources for improving writing skills.

Looking for all genres.

Representative Articles
- The View From Downstairs
- The She Ruler
- The Humidity of Night

How to Get Connected

Contact:
R. James Stahl, Editor

Accepts articles by: ☒ Email ☐ Fax ☐ Phone ☐ Letter
See submission guidelines online.

Email: Merlyn@merlynspen.org

Web Site: http://www.merlynspen.org

New Moon

2 West 1st Street, #101, Duluth, MN 55802
(800) 381 4743

What They Publish

Publishes stories for every girl who wants her voice heard and her dreams taken seriously, and for every adult who cares about girls.

Looking for articles by girls 8–14 about women in history, interesting women or girls, and girls from around the world. Also publishes fiction, poetry, and artwork by girls.

Representative Articles

- Beautiful Girls Issue
- Weird, Wacky and Random Issue
- Fantasies and Fairytales Issue

How to Get Connected

Contact:
Kate Freeborn, Executive Editor

Accepts articles by: ☒ Email ☐ Fax ☐ Phone ☒ Letter
See submission guidelines online.

Email:

Web Site: http://www.newmoon.org

Potluck Magazine

PO Box 546, Deerfield, IL 60015
(847) 948 1139

What They Publish

Publishes poetry, short stories, fables, book reviews, and artwork by young writers and artist ages 8-16.

Looking for poetry, book reviews, short stories, and artwork.

Representative Articles
-
-

How to Get Connected

Contact:
Susan Napoli Picchietti, Editor in Chief

Accepts articles by: ☒ Email ☐ Fax   ☐ Phone ☒ Letter
See submission guidelines online.

Email: submissions@potluckmagazine.org

Web Site: http://www.potluckmagazine.org

Skipping Stones

PO Box 3939, Eugene OR 97403-0939
(541) 342 4956

What They Publish

Publishes multicultural stories for youth and adult market.

Looking for essays, stories, letters to the editor, riddles and proverbs.

Representative Articles
- Tibetan Students Share Their Culture and Daily Life
- Tan, I Am: Being Biracial
- No School for a Year! Learning on the Road

How to Get Connected

Contact:
Managing Editor

Accepts articles by: ☒ Email ☐ Fax ☐ Phone ☒ Letter
See submission guidelines and ideas for submissions online.

Email: editor@skippingstones.org

Web Site: http://www.skippingstones.org

Stone Soup

PO Box 83 Santa Cruz, CA 95063
(800) 477 4569

What They Publish

Publishes stories, poems, book reviews, and art by young people through age 13.

Looking for stories and poems about the things you feel most strongly about! Whether your work is about imaginary situations or real ones, use your own experiences and observations to give your work depth and a sense of reality.

Representative Articles
- Hall of Fame
- Make the Morning
- Crippled Detectives

How to Get Connected

Contact:
Gerry Madel, Publisher and Editor
William Rubel, Publisher and Editor

Accepts articles by: ☐ Email ☐ Fax ☐ Phone ☒ Letter
See submission guidelines online.

Email: editor@stonesoup.com

Web Site: http://www.stonesoup.com

Teen Magazine

Hearst Magazines
3000 Ocean Park Boulevard, Suite 3048, Santa Monica, CA 90405
(310) 664 2950

What They Publish

Monthly magazine for a junior high school female audience.

Looking for all types of stories, but query only. Will not accept unsolicited submissions.

Representative Articles
- Make Extra Cash This Summer
- Find Your Flirting Style
- All in the Family—One Girl's Story of Adoption

How to Get Connected

Contact:
Jane Fort, Editor in Chief
Kelly Bryant, Entertainment Editor
Heather Hewitt, Managing Editor

Accepts articles by: ☐ Email ☐ Fax ☐ Phone ☐ Letter
Query only.

Email:

Web Site: http://www.teenmag.com

Teen Voices

PO Box 120-027, Boston, MA 02112-0027
(888) 882 TEEN

What They Publish

Publishes stories by, for, and about teenage and young adult women.

Looking for writing, art, and stories of personal activism from girls 13–19.

Representative Articles

- Art & Soul: Talented Teens Share Their Inspiration
- A Girl's Rite of Way: Stepping into Womanhood
- From Prissy to Powerful: Taking Back the Color Pink

How to Get Connected

Contact:
Editor

Accepts articles by: ☒ Email ☐ Fax   ☐ Phone ☒ Letter
See submission guidelines online.

Email:

Web Site: http://www.teenvoices.com

Twist

270 Sylvan Avenue, Englewood Cliffs, NJ 07632

What They Publish

Publishes stories reflecting the teen experience.

Looking for stories and input for features. Topics change monthly. See website for details.

Representative Articles
- Entertainment
- Celeb Scoop
- Style Zone

How to Get Connected

Contact:
Editor

Accepts articles by: ☒ Email ☐ Fax ☐ Phone ☒ Letter
See submission guidelines online.

Email: twistmail@twistmagazine.com

Web Site: http://www.twistmagazine.com

Read, Write, Listen

Read as many of the great books as you can
before the age of 22.
—James Michener

It is by sitting down to write every morning
that one becomes a writer.
Those who do not do this remain amateurs.
—Gerald Brown

The discipline of the writer
is to learn to be still and listen
to what his subject has to tell him.
—Rachel Carson

Online Writing Sites & Local Programs

Here are some Internet sites for young writers. Many of them are sites that publish work by young writers; others provide resource information on writing or getting published; some do both. All are worth a look.

826Chicago

1331 North Milwaukee Avenue, Chicago, IL 60622
826CHI is a non-profit organization dedicated to supporting students ages 6 to 18 with their creative and expository writing skills, and to helping teachers inspire their students to write.
www.826CHI.org

ChicagoWriter

This site provides information on books, resources, and programs specifically for Chicago-area writers.
www.ChicagoWriter.com

CyberKids

Site for writers under the age of 12 to share stories, poetry, art, and articles.
www.CyberKids.com

Cyberteens

Site for teenage writers to share stories, poetry, art, and information.
www.CyberTeens.com

Diary Project

This site encourages teens to write about their day-to-day experiences growing up. There are thousands of entries in 24 categories posted on the site.
www.DiaryProject.com

Free Street

1419 West Blackhawk, 3rd Floor, Chicago, IL 60622
Free Street opens the potential of youth through theater and writing to be creative, active participants in their own destiny. Youth (with a focus on teens) participate in long term workshops which help to cultivate better habits for curious learning and passionate living. Workshops lead to the creation of performances or books.
www.freestreet.org

GirlZone

A webzine for teenage girls. Has opportunities for writing, art, and internships.
www.GirlZone.com

Guild Complex

1212 North Ashland, Suite 211, Chicago, IL 60622
The Guild Complex is an independent, not for profit cultural center that serves as a forum for literary cross cultural expression, discussion and education in combination with other arts. We believe that the arts are instrumental in defining and exploring the human experience, while encouraging participation by artist and audience alike in changing the conditions of our society.
www.GuildComplex.com

NaNoWriMo's Young Writer's Program

November is National Novel Writing Month (NaNoWriMo) and young writers are invited to participate.
www.ywp.nanowrimo.org/

The Scriptorium

Scriptorium means a room set apart for writing. On this site you will find articles, interviews, exercises, book reviews, and more to help you become the best writer you can be. Also has a special page for young writers.
www.TheScriptorium.com

Teen Lit

Teens can submit poetry, essays, short stories, and book reviews for publication on the site. They also have information and advice about how to improve your writing and how to get published.
www.TeenLit.com

Teen Writer's and Artist's Project

An Illinois Non-Profit corporation formed to supply a resource for writers and artists, ages 14–18, to obtain training and support in their craft, for example: creative writing, journalism, painting, photography, etc.
http://teenwritersandartistsproject.blogspot.com/

Writing.com

This site is an online community for writers and readers of all interests and skill levels. Membership is free.
www.Writing.com

Young Chicago Authors

2049 West Division, 2nd Floor, Chicago, IL 60622
YCA provides student-centered, artist-led workshops free to youth ages 13-19 in schools and communities.
www.YoungChicagoAuthors.org

Young Writers' Clubhouse

Learn more about the craft of writing, meet real authors, and even join a critique group.
www.RealKids.com/club.shtml

Young Writer's Network

This site showcases writing by authors ages 18 and under. It also provides information on markets and contests for young writers.
www.YoungWriterNetwork.com

The Young Writers Society

This site was specifically created for young writers to share their work with each other.
www.YoungWritersSociety.com

Imagination and Inspiration

Many characters have come to me...in a dream,
and then I'll elaborate from there.
I always write down all my dreams.
—William Burroughs

When I sit at my table to write, I never know what
it's going to be till I'm under way.
I trust in inspiration, which sometimes comes and
sometimes doesn't. But I don't sit back waiting for it.
I work *every* day.
—Alberto Moravia

I don't wait to be struck by lightning
and don't need certain slants of light in order to write.
—Toni Morrison

Contests

If you're an enterprising young writer with a taste for competition, you might want to try entering a contest or two. In general, we do not recommend those contests that require hefty entrance fees, but if the topic is your specialty and the payoff is high enough, it could be worth a try. Be sure to contact the organization or visit their web site for details and entry forms.

AIM Magazine Short Story Contest

AIM Publishing Company, PO Box 1174, Maywood, IL 60153-8174
http://www.aimmagazine.org
Awarded for well-written stories with lasting social significance proving that people from differing backgrounds are more alike than they are different. Maximum length is 4,000 words. Award: $100.
Closing Date: August 15

The Nelson Algren Awards

Chicago Tribune, 435 N. Michigan Avenue, Chicago, IL 60611
http://www.chicagotribune.com
Awarded for outstanding unpublished story by an American writer. Manuscript must be 2,500–10,000 words in length. Award: $5,000.
Closing Date: February 1

Arts Recognitions and Talent Search (ARTS)

National Foundation for Advancement in the Arts
800 Bricknall Avenue, Suite 500, Miami, FL 33131
http://www.artsawards.org
Scholarship opportunities to 17–18 arts students with demonstrated talent in dance, jazz, film, visual arts, and writing. Award: up to $10,000.
Closing Date: June 1

Vincent Astor Memorial Leadership Essay Contest

291 Wood Road, Annapolis, MD 21402
http://www.navalinstitute.org
Essay contest on naval leadership (3,500 words).
Award: $1,500 and gold medal.
Closing Date: February 15

AWP Award Series

Associated Writing Programs
George Mason University, MS-1E3, Fairfax, VA 22030
http://www.awpwriter.org
An open competition for book-length manuscript in: poetry, short fiction,
novel, and creative nonfiction. Award: $2,000 and publication.
Closing Date: February 28

Basile Festival of Emerging American Theatre

The Phoenix Theatre, 749 N. Park Avenue, Indianapolis, IN 46202
http://www.phoenixtheatre.org
Open playwriting contest. Award: $1,000.
Closing Date: February 28

Susan Smith Blackburn Prize

3239 Avalon Place, Houston, TX 77019
Awarded to an English-speaking woman for outstanding full-length play
written in English. Award: $10,000.
Closing Date: September 30

Barbara Bradley Prize

New England Poetry Club, 137 W. Newton Street, Boston, MA 02118
http://www.nepoetryclub.org
Awarded for poem in lyric form, fewer than 21 lines, written by a woman.
Award: $200.
Closing Date: June 30

Gerald Cable Book Award

Silverfish Review Press, PO Box 3541, Eugene, OR 97403
SFRpress@aol.com
Awarded for best poetry book by an author who has not yet published a
collection. Award: $1,000 and publication.
Closing Date: December 1

Raymond Carver Short Story Contest

English Department/Humboldt State University
One Harpst Street, Arcata, CA 95521
carver@humboldt.edu
Open short story contest. Award: $1,000.
Closing Date: June 10

Cunningham Commission for Youth Theatre
The Theatre School
DePaul University, 2135 N Kenmore, Chicago, IL 60614
http://www.theatreschool.depaul.edu
Open playwriting contest. Award: $5,000 and publication.
Closing Date: December 1

Delacorte Press Prize for a First Young Adult Novel
Delacorte Press Books, 1540 Broadway, New York NY 10036
http://www.randomhouse.com/kids
Awarded for book length mss and summary suitable for readers 12–18,
100–224 pages. Open to American writers who have not previously
published a young adult novel. Award: $1,500 + $6,000 advance against
royalties.
Closing Date: postmarked between October 1–December 31

Eaton Literary Associates Literary Awards
Eaton Literary Agency Inc., PO Box 49795, Sarasota, FL 34230-6795
http://www.eatonliterary.com
Two awards: one for book-length manuscript and one for a short story or
article. Entries should not have been previously published. Award: $2,500
book, $500 short story or article.
Closing Date: August 31, book; March 31, short story or article

Foster City Writers Contest
Foster City Arts & Cultural Committee
650 Shell Boulevard, Foster City, CA 94404
http://www.fostercity.com
Awarded for fiction, humor, children's story and poetry, personal essay,
rhymed verse, and blank verse. Entries must be original, previously
unpublished, and in English. Award: $250 in each category.
Closing Date: October 31

Guideposts Young Writers Contest
Guideposts Books and Inspirational Media Division
16 East 34th Street, New York, NY 10016
http://www.guidepostbooks.com
Youth writing contest open to high school juniors and seniors.
Award: $10,000.
Closing Date: November 24

Handy Andy Prize

> The Poetry Society of Virginia, 100 N. Berwick, Williamsburg, VA 23188
> http://www.poetrysocietyofvirginia.org
> Awarded for outstanding limerick. Award: $25.
> Closing Date: January 15

L Ron Hubbard's Writers of the Future Contest

> PO Box 1630, Los Angeles, CA 90078
> contests@authorservicesinc.com http://www.writersofthefuture.com
> Awarded for short stories and novelettes of science fiction and fantasy for
> new and amateur writers.
> Award: $1,000 quarterly, $4,000 annual grand prize.
> Closing Date: December 31, March 31, June 30, and September 30

Juniper Prize for Poetry

> University of Massachusetts Press
> PO Box 429, Amherst, MA 01004
> maldonado@umpress.umass.edu http://www.umass.edu/umpress
> Awarded for poetry manuscripts that haven't been published.
> Award: $1,000 and publication.
> Closing Date: September 30

Coretta Scott King Awards

> Social Responsibilities Round Table, American Library Association
> 50 West Huron Street, Chicago, IL 60611
> http://www.ala.org/srrt/csking
> Awarded to encourage the artistic expression of African-American
> experiences via literature and the graphic arts. Award: $1,000, seal on
> book and set of encyclopedia.
> Closing Date: December 1

McLaren Memorial Comedy Playwriting Competition

> Midland Community Theatre, 2000 W. Wadley, Midland, TX 79705
> http://www.mctmidland.org
> An open competition for unproduced comedy scripts.
> Award: $300 full-length play; $100 one-act play.
> Closing Date: January

Milkweed National Fiction Prize

> Milkweed Editions,
> 1011 Washington Avenue South, Suite 300, Minneapolis, MN 55415
> http://www.milkweed.org
> Awarded for unpublished novel or collection of short stories or novellas.
> Award: $5,000 advance and publication.
> Closing Date: Ongoing

National Ten-Minute Play Contest

Actors Theatre of Louisville, 316 W. Main Street, Louisville, KY 40202
http://www.actorstheatre.org
An open ten-page playwriting contest. Award: $1,000.
Closing Date: December 1

National Writers Association Novel Contest

National Writers Association
3140 S. Peoria Street, Suite 295, Aurora, CO 80014
http://www.nationalwriters.com
An open contest for novel-length manuscripts. Award: $500.
Closing Date: April 1

North American Indian Prose Award

University of Nebraska Press
233 N. 8th Street, Lincoln, NE 68588
http://www.nebraskapress.unl.edu
Awarded for complete mss in prose nonfiction. Authors must be American
Indians. Award: $1,000 advance against royalties.
Closing Date: July 1

The Flannery O'Connor Award for Short Fiction

University of Georgia Press
330 Research Drive, Athens, GA 30602
http://www.uga.edu/ugapress
Awarded for collections of short fiction. Manuscripts should be 200–275
pages. Award: $1,000.
Closing Date: May 31

Playboy College Fiction Contest

Playboy Enterprises Inc., 680 N. Lake Shore Drive, Chicago IL 60611
http://www.playboy.com
Short story contest for accredited college/university students.
Award: $3,000 and publication.
Closing Date: December 31

Poetry In Print

1 Poetry Plaza, Owings Mills, MD 21117
http://www.poetry.com
Open poetry contest. Award: $1,000.
Closing Date: Ongoing.

Katherine Anne Porter Prize

Nimrod, The University of Tulsa, 600 S. College, Tulsa, OK 74104
nimrod@utulsa.edu http://www.utulsa.edu/nimrod
Open writing contest of 7,500 words maximum. Award: $2,000.
Closing Date: April 30

River City Writing Awards in Fiction

Hohenburg Foundation, Department of English
Memphis University, Memphis, TN 38152
rivercity@memphis.edu
http://www.people.memphis.edu/~rivercity/contests.html
Awarded to any previously unpublished short story of up to 7,500 words.
Award: $1,500.
Closing Date: March 15

Nicholas Roerich Poetry Prize

Story Line Press, P.O. Box 1240, Ashland, OR 97520
mail@storylinepress.com http://www.storylinepress.com
First book contest for an unpublished manuscript of poetry. Award:
$1,000. Closing Date: October 31

The Barbara Savage Award

The Mountaineers Books
1001 SW Klickitat Way, Suite 201, Seattle, WA 98134
mbooks@mountaineers.org http://www.mountaineersbooks.org
Awarded for compelling nonfiction account of a personal outdoor
adventure. Acceptable subjects include personal narratives involving
hiking, mountain climbing, bicycling, paddle sports, skiing, snowshoeing,
nature, conservations, ecology, and adventure travel not based on
motorized transport. Award: $3,000.
Closing Date: March 1

Seventeen Magazine Fiction Contest

Hearst Corporation, 1440 Broadway, 13th Floor, New York, NY 10018
http://www.seventeen.com
Fiction writing contest open to 13–21 year olds. Submission must be
1500–3500 words and previously unpublished. Award: $1,000 and
publication. Closing Date: April 30

Dorothy Silver Playwriting Competition

Jewish Community Theater of Cleveland
3505 Mayfield Road, Cleveland Heights, OH 44118
http://www.clevejcc.org
Open playwriting contest for plays with a Jewish theme. Award: $1,000,
plus staged reading.
Closing Date: May 31

Agnes Lynch Starrett Poetry Prize

University of Pittsburgh Press
3400 Forbes Avenue, Pittsburgh, PA 15260
http://www.pitt.edu/~press
Open to any poet who has not had a full-length book previously
published. Award: $5,000 and publication.
Closing Date: April 30

Daniel Varoujan Award

New England Poetry Club, 137 W. Newton Street, Boston, MA 02118
http://www.nepoetryclub.org
Awarded for an unpublished poem in English worthy of the Armenian poet
executed by the Turks in 1915 at the onset of the genocide of the
Armenian population. Award: $1,000.
Closing Date June 30

Theodore Ward Prize for Playwriting

Columbia College, Theater Department,
72 E. 11th Street, Chicago, IL 60605
chigochuck@aol.com http://www.colum.edu
Awarded for full-length play by an African-American playwright.
Award: $2,000.
Closing Date: July 1

White Bird Annual Playwriting Contest

White Bird Productions Inc.
138 S. Oxford Street, Suite 2-B, Brooklyn, NY 11217
Open playwriting contest for best play that deals with an environmental
issue, plot, or theme. Award: $200 and NYC reading.
Closing Date: March 15

Walt Whitman Award

Academy of America Poets Inc.
588 Broadway, Suite 1203, New York, NY 10012
academy@poets.org http://www.poets.org
Awarded for a book-length manuscript of poetry by a living American poet
who has not published a book of poetry. Award: $5,000 and publication.
Closing Date: September 15–November 15

Justin Winsor Prize Essay

Library History Round Table, American Library Association
50 East Huron Street, Chicago, IL 60611
alsc@ala.org http://www.ala.org/alaorg/ors/winsor.html
Awarded to the author of an outstanding essay embodying original historical research on a significant subject of library history.
Award: $500 and publication.
Closing Date: February 1

Paul A. Witty Short Story Award

International Reading Association, 800 Barksdale Road, Newark, DE 19711
http://www.reading.org
Awarded for an original story published for the first time for children. The story should serve as a literary standard that encourages young readers to read periodicals. Award: $1,000.
Closing Date: December 1

Thomas Wolfe Student Prize

Thomas Wolfe Society, 809 Gardner Street, Raleigh, NC 27607
http://www.thomaswolfe.org
Awarded for an outstanding essay related to Thomas Wolfe and his work.
Award: $500, publication, and one year membership in the Society.
Closing Date: January 15

Word Works Washington Prize

The Word Works, P.O. Box 42164, Washington, DC 20015
editor@wordworks.com
Awarded for an unpublished manuscript of poetry by a living American writer. Award: $1,500 and publication.
Closing Date: March 1

World's Best Short Story Contest

The Southeast Review, Department of English
The Florida State University, 405 Williams Building, Tallahassee, FL 32306
http://www.english.fsu.edu
Awarded to the best 300-word maximum previously unpublished short story. Award: $300 and a box of Florida oranges.
Closing Date: April 15

Writer's Journal Annual Fiction Contest

Val-Tech Media, P.O. Box 394, Perham, MN 56573
writersjournal@lakesplus.com http://www.writersjournal.com
Open contest for unpublished works of fiction not to exceed 2,000 words.
Award: $50.
Closing Date: January 30

Writer's Journal Annual Horror/Ghost Contest

Val-Tech Media, P.O. Box 394, Perham, MN 56573
writersjournal@lakesplus.com http://www.writersjournal.com
Open contest for unpublished works of fiction in horror genre not to
exceed 2,000 words. Award: $50.
Closing Date: March 30

Writer's Journal Annual Romance Contest

Val-Tech Media, P.O. Box 394, Perham, MN 56573
writersjournal@lakesplus.com http://www.writersjournal.com
Open contest for unpublished works of fiction in romance genre not to
exceed 2,000 words. Award: $50.
Closing Date: July 30

Writer's Journal Annual Short Story Contest

Val-Tech Media, P.O. Box 394, Perham, MN 56573
writersjournal@lakesplus.com http://www.writersjournal.com
Open contest for unpublished short stories not to exceed 2,000 words.
Award: $50.
Closing Date: May 30

Writer's Journal Annual Poetry Contest

Val-Tech Media, P.O. Box 394, Perham, MN 56573
writersjournal@lakesplus.com http://www.writersjournal.com
Open contest for unpublished poems not to exceed 25 lines. Award: $25.
Closing Date: December 30

Yale Series of Younger Poets

Yale University Press
302 Temple Street, New Haven, CT 06511
http://www.yale.edu/yup
Awarded for outstanding poetry by American writers under age 40 who
have not previously had a volume of verse published. Award: Publication
and royalties.
Closing Date: January 1–31

Competition

I don't feel in competition with other writers.
Because I don't write about the same things as any other
writer that I know of does.
—Truman Capote

I can write better than anyone who can write faster,
and I can write faster than anyone who can write better.
—A.J. Liebling

Writing...is practically the only activity a person can do
that is not competitive.
—Paul Theroux

College Writing Programs

This section details college writing programs in the Chicago area. The programs will give you an idea of the many directions your writing can take.

Many of these institutions have summer and weekend programs for high school juniors and seniors who have a proven ability to write. (Some may even allow you to take college-level classes on a part-time basis.)

If you are interested in any of the college programs, contact the college's admissions personnel and talk the matter over with your school college admissions counselor.

Benedictine University

Specifics

Entrance Requirements: SAT: 990   ACT: 21   HS GPA: 3.0

Degreed Writing Programs: Communication Arts

Sample Class Titles: Technical Writing • Public Relations Writing •
Writing for the Electronic Media • Editing for Publication • Advertising
Copywriting • Layout and Design for Publication • Newswriting and
Reporting

Instructor/Student Ratio: **Average Class Size**: 20
92 FT + 128 PT / 1,930 (1:9)

Success Stories

% of Students Who Go on to Graduate Study:
Notable Writers From Faculty/Alumni:

Contact Information

Kari Crammer, Dean of Undergraduate Admissions
Benedictine University
5700 College Road, Lisle, IL 60532
(630) 829 6300

admissions@ben.edu
http://www.ben.edu

Chicago State University

Specifics

Entrance Requirements:　SAT:　　ACT: 16–19　　HS GPA: 2.0

Degreed Writing Programs:　English/Rhetoric • Business and Technical Writing

Sample Class Titles: Writing and Editing Nonfiction • Elements of Literary Study and Research Writing • Critical Strategies for Writing and Research • Writing in African American Literature • Language • Advanced Research Methods

Instructor/Student Ratio:　　　　　　　　**Average Class Size**: 30
 329 FT + 110 PT / 4,870　(1:11)

Success Stories

% of Students Who Go on to Graduate Study: 2%
Notable Writers From Faculty/Alumni:
 Gwendolyn Brooks • Haki Madhubuti

Contact Information

Addie Epps, Director of Admissions
Chicago State University
9501 South King Drive, Chicago, IL 60628
(773) 995 2513
ug-admissions@csu.edu
http://www.csu.edu

Concordia University

Specifics

Entrance Requirements: SAT: ACT: 20   HS GPA:

Degreed Writing Programs: Communications • English

Sample Class Titles: Writing About Media • Writing About Theology • Writing About Literature • Business Communication • Broadcast and Print Journalism • Writing Style and Strategy

Instructor/Student Ratio: **Average Class Size**: 20
   78 FT + 60 PT / 1,171 (1:8)

Success Stories

%of Students Who Go on to Graduate Study: 8%
Notable Writers From Faculty/Alumni:

Contact Information

Michelle Mega, Director of Undergraduate Admissions
Concordia University
7400 Augusta Street, River Forest, IL 60305
(708) 209 3100
crfadmis@curf.edu
http://www.curf.edu

DePaul University

Specifics

Entrance Requirements: SAT: 1000–1230   ACT: 21–27   HS GPA: 3.0

Degreed Writing Programs: Communication • Playwriting • English/Creative Writing • English/Professional Writing

Sample Class Titles: Editing • Writing for Public Communication • Screenwriting • Feature Writing • Grammar and Usage • Rhetorical Criticism • Interviewing • Writing in the Professions • News Writing • Speechwriting and Presentation • Literary Research and Writing • Public Relations Writing • Fiction Writing • Poetry Writing • Composition and Style • Corporate Communication • Business and Professional Communication • Academic Writing • Technical Writing • Rhetoric • Stylistics

Instructor/Student Ratio: **Average Class Size**: 20
785 FT + 1423 PT / 13,801 (1:6)

Success Stories

%of Students Who Go on to Graduate Study: 30%
Notable Writers From Faculty/Alumni: Richard Jones

Contact Information

Carlene Klass, Director of Undergraduate Admissions
DePaul University
1 East Jackson Boulevard, Chicago, IL 60604
(312) 362 8300
admitdpu@depaul.edu
http://www.depaul.edu

Dominican University

Specifics

Entrance Requirements: SAT: ACT: 20 or above HS GPA: 2.75 minimum

Degreed Writing Programs: Communications • Business and Technical Writing

Sample Class Titles: Writing Nonfiction Prose • Autobiography • Business Writing

Instructor/Student Ratio: **Average Class Size**: 15
   89 FT + 115 PT / 1,092 (1:12)

Success Stories

Percentage of Students Who Go on to Graduate Study: 25%
Notable Writers From Faculty/Alumni:

Contact Information

Pamela Johnson, Vice President for Enrollment
Dominican University
7900 West Division, River Forest, IL 60305
(708) 524 6800
domadmis@dom.edu
http://www.dom.edu

East West University

Specifics

Entrance Requirements: SAT: ACT: HS GPA:

Degreed Writing Programs: English • Communications

Sample Class Titles: Writing From Sources • Persuasion and Research • Business Communication • Technical Writing • Rhetoric and Style • Desktop Publishing • Basic News Writing • Literature for Children • Creative Writing • Advanced Composition

Instructor/Student Ratio: **Average Class Size**: 20
14 FT + 65 PT / 1,113 (1:14)

Success Stories

%of Students Who Go on to Graduate Study:
Notable Writers From Faculty/Alumni:

Contact Information

William Link, Director of Admissions
East West University
816 South Michigan Avenue, Chicago, IL 60605
(312) 939 0111
seeyou@eastwest.edu
http://www.eastwest.edu

Elmhurst College

Specifics

Entrance Requirements: SAT: ACT: 19–26   HS GPA: 3.0

Degreed Writing Programs:
English/Writing

Sample Class Titles: Composition • Principles of Literary Study • News Writing • Writing in the Professional Fields • Feature Writing • Writing Fiction • Advanced Writing • Principles of Interviewing

Instructor/Student Ratio: **Average Class Size**: 19
   113 FT + 150 PT / 2,269 (1:9)

Success Stories

%of Students Who Go on to Graduate Study: 37%
Notable Writers From Faculty/Alumni:

Contact Information

Andrew Sison, Director of Admissions
Elmhurst College
190 Prospect Avenue, Elmhurst, IL 60126
(630) 617 3400
admit@elmhurst.edu
http://www.elmhurst.edu

Governors State University

Specifics

Entrance Requirements: SAT: - ACT: - HS GPA: -

Degreed Writing Programs: Media • English/Writing

Sample Class Titles: Business Communication • Research Writing • Instructional Design Basics • Composition • Writing Principles • Linguistics • Modern English Grammar • Writing for Print Media • News Writing • Trends in Communication Techniques • Writing Theory and Practice

Instructor/Student Ratio: 175 FT + 29 PT / 2,980 (1:15)

Average Class Size: 30

Success Stories

%of Students Who Go on to Graduate Study:
Notable Writers From Faculty/Alumni:

Contact Information

Larry Polselli, Director of Admissions
Governors State University
University Parkway, University Park, IL 60466
(708) 534 4490
gsunow@govst.edu
http://www.govst.edu

Judson College

Specifics

Entrance Requirements: SAT: 860   ACT: 18 HS GPA: 2.0

Degreed Writing Programs: English • Media Studies

Sample Class Titles: Advanced Writing • Research Methods •
Philosophy of Language

Instructor/Student Ratio: **Average Class Size**: 20
   55 FT + 68 PT / 1,153 (1:9)

Success Stories

%of Students Who Go on to Graduate Study:
Notable Writers From Faculty/Alumni:

Contact Information

William Dean, Director of Admissions
Judson College
1151 North State Street, Elgin, IL 60123
(847) 628 2510
admissions@judsoncollege.edu
http://www.judsoncollege.edu

Lake Forest College

Specifics

Entrance Requirements: SAT: 1030–1240   ACT: 23–28 HS GPA: 3.0

Degreed Writing Programs: Communications • English

Sample Class Titles: Argumentative Writing and Speaking • Magazine Writing • American Nature Writing • Creative Writing • Nonfiction Writing • Poetry Writing • Playwriting

Instructor/Student Ratio: **Average Class Size**: 20
  87 FT + 59 PT / 1,289 (1:8)

Success Stories

%of Students Who Go on to Graduate Study: 39%
Notable Writers From Faculty/Alumni:
Davis Schneiderman (novelist) • Robert Archambeau (poet) • Ralph Mills, Jr. (poet) • Phillip Simmons

Contact Information

William Motzer, Director of Admissions
Lake Forest College
555 North Sheridan Road, Lake Forest, IL 60045
(847) 735 5000
admissions@lakeforest.edu
http://www.lakeforest.edu

Loyola University of Chicago

Specifics

Entrance Requirements: SAT: 1040–1270   ACT: 22–27 HS GPA:

Degreed Writing Programs: Communications • English

Sample Class Titles: Broadcast News • Radio/TV Writing • Copy Editing • Feature and Opinion Writing • Layout and Editing • Writing for Business and Trade Publications • Investigative Reporting • Criticism and Theory • Fiction • Grammar • Poetry • Advanced Writing Workshop • Business Writing

Instructor/Student Ratio: **Average Class Size**: 40
  940 FT + 1039 PT / 6,821 (1:13)

Success Stories

%of Students Who Go on to Graduate Study: 30%
Notable Writers From Faculty/Alumni:
Allen Frantzen • Pamela L. Caughie • David M. Posner

Contact Information

April Hansen, Director of Admissions
Loyola University of Chicago
820 North Michigan Avenue, Chicago, IL 60611
(312) 915 6500
admission@luc.edu
http://www.luc.edu

National-Louis University

Specifics

Entrance Requirements: SAT: 750   ACT: 19 HS GPA:

Degreed Writing Programs: English/Composition

Sample Class Titles: Composition • Creative Writing • Language and Linguistics • Rhetorical Theory

Instructor/Student Ratio: **Average Class Size**: 20
282 FT + 0 PT / 3,043 (1:11)

Success Stories

%of Students Who Go on to Graduate Study: 8%
Notable Writers From Faculty/Alumni:

Contact Information

Patricia Petillo, Director of Admissions
National-Louis University
122 South Michigan Avenue, Chicago, IL 60603
(312) 475 1100
nluinfo@wheeling1.nl.edu
http://www.nl.edu

North Central College

Specifics

Entrance Requirements: SAT: 1040–1250   ACT: 20–27 HS GPA: 3.0

Degreed Writing Programs: English/Writing • Broadcast Communications

Sample Class Titles: contact college for full course catalog

Instructor/Student Ratio: **Average Class Size**: 20
 125 FT + 71 PT / 1,986 (1:21)

Success Stories

%of Students Who Go on to Graduate Study: 13%
Notable Writers From Faculty/Alumni:

Contact Information

Marguerite Waters, Director of Admissions
North Central College
30 North Brainard Street, Naperville, IL 60566
(630) 637 5800
ncadm@noctrl.edu
http://www.noctrl.edu

North Park University

Specifics

Entrance Requirements: SAT: 1000–1270   ACT: 18–25 HS GPA:

Degreed Writing Programs: Communication Arts • English/Writing

Sample Class Titles: Composition • Writing for Mass Media • Dramatic Writing • Journalism • Grammar and Writing Pedagogy • Writing Fiction • Writing Poetry • Advanced Writing • Rhetorical Criticism • Media Writing • Copywriting

Instructor/Student Ratio: **Average Class Size**: 20
  72 FT + 127 PT / 1,584 (1:8)

Success Stories

%of Students Who Go on to Graduate Study: Departments do not currently track that information.

Notable Writers From Faculty/Alumni: Kristy Odelius

Contact Information

Mark Olson, Dean of Enrollment
North Park University
3225 West Foster Avenue, Chicago, IL 60625
(773) 244 5500
admission@northpark.edu
http://www.northpark.edu

Northeastern Illinois University

Specifics

Entrance Requirements: SAT: 890   ACT: 19 HS GPA: 2.0

Degreed Writing Programs:
English/Writing

Sample Class Titles: Writing in Context • Creative Writing • Written
Communication for Business • Writing for Public Relations and
Advertising • Argumentative Prose • Poetry • Fiction • Advanced
Composition

Instructor/Student Ratio: **Average Class Size**: 30
 370 FT + 253 PT / 2,121 (1:3)

Success Stories

%of Students Who Go on to Graduate Study: 20%
Notable Writers From Faculty/Alumni:

Contact Information

Miriam Rivera, Director of Admissions
Northeastern Illinois University
5500 North St. Louis Avenue, Chicago, IL 60625
(773) 442 4000
admit@neiu.edu
http://www.neiu.edu

Northwestern University

Specifics

Entrance Requirements: SAT: 1300–1480   ACT: 28–33 HS GPA:

Degreed Writing Programs: English/Writing • Journalism • Communication

Sample Class Titles: Newswriting and Reporting • Magazine Writing • Literary Journalism • Practical Rhetoric • Composition • Poetry • Theory and Practice of Fiction

Instructor/Student Ratio: **Average Class Size**: 20
922 FT + 220 PT / 7,875 (1:9)

Success Stories

%of Students Who Go on to Graduate Study: 28%
Notable Writers From Faculty/Alumni:
Saul Bellow (Nobel Prize in Literature) • Robert Olen Butler (Pulitzer Prize in Literature) • Bruce Dold (Pulitzer Prize in Journalism) • Jack Fuller (Pulitzer Prize in Journalism) • Georgie Anne Geyer (national syndicated columnist) • Julia Wallace (editor, *Atlanta Journal-Constitution*)

Contact Information

Keith Todd, Director of Undergraduate Admissions
Northwestern University
1801 Hinman Avenue, Evanston, IL 60208
(847) 491 4100
ug-admission@northwestern.edu
http://www.northwestern.edu

Roosevelt University

Specifics

Entrance Requirements: SAT: ACT: 16–20 HS GPA:

Degreed Writing Programs: English/Composition • Journalism •
Professional Communications

Sample Class Titles: Business Communications • Global
Communications • News Reporting and Writing • Editing • Composition
• Style and Grammar • Writing About Ideas • Literary Analysis •
Creative Writing • Professional Writing • Fiction Writing • Poetry Writing
• Play Writing • Creative Nonfiction • Nonfiction Writing • Screenwriting •
Literary Magazine Industry

Instructor/Student Ratio: **Average Class Size**: 30
 182 FT + 414 PT / 4,200 (1:7)

Success Stories

%of Students Who Go on to Graduate Study:
Notable Writers From Faculty/Alumni:

Contact Information

Brian Lynch, Director of Admissions
Roosevelt University
430 South Michigan Avenue, Chicago, IL 60605
(312) 341 3515
applyru@roosevelt.edu
http://www.roosevelt.edu

St. Xavier University

Specifics

Entrance Requirements: SAT: ACT: 19–24 HS GPA: 2.5

Degreed Writing Programs: Communication • English

Sample Class Titles: Media Writing • Newswriting and Reporting • Scriptwriting for Television and Film • Advertising Copywriting • Business and Professional Writing • Persuasion

Instructor/Student Ratio: (1:16)   **Average Class Size**: 30

Success Stories

%of Students Who Go on to Graduate Study: 9%
Notable Writers From Faculty/Alumni:

Contact Information

Beth Glerach, Managing Director of Enrollment
St. Xavier University
3700 West 103rd Street, Chicago, IL 60655
(773) 298 3050
admissions@sxu.edu
http://www.sxu.edu

Trinity Christian College

Specifics

Entrance Requirements: SAT: 950–1220   ACT: 20–26   HS GPA: 3.0

Degreed Writing Programs: Business Communication • English

Sample Class Titles: Journalism • Advanced Writing • Screenwriting • Professional Communication • Public Relations • Web Page Design • Composition • Linguistics • Honors Writing • Advanced Writing

Instructor/Student Ratio: **Average Class Size**: 20
56 FT + 54 PT / 968 (1:9)

Success Stories

%of Students Who Go on to Graduate Study: 13%
Notable Writers From Faculty/Alumni:

Contact Information

Pete Hamstra, Vice President Admissions
Trinity Christian College
6601 West College Drive, Palos Heights, IL 60463
(708) 239 4708
adm@trnty.edu
http://www.trnty.edu

Trinity International University

Specifics

Entrance Requirements: SAT: 930–1140   ACT: 19–25 HS GPA: 2.5

Degreed Writing Programs: English/Communication

Sample Class Titles: Writing for Media • Desktop Publishing • Business Communication • Creative Writing • Mass Communications

Instructor/Student Ratio: **Average Class Size**: 20
40 FT + 47 PT / 1,162 (1:13)

Success Stories

%of Students Who Go on to Graduate Study: 20%
Notable Writers From Faculty/Alumni:
Cliff Williams • Daniel Song'ony • Kristin Lindholm

Contact Information

Matt Yoder, Director of Admissions
Trinity International University
2065 Half Day Road, Deerfield, IL 60015
(847) 317 7000
tcdadm@tiu.edu
http://www.tiu.edu

University of Chicago

Specifics

Entrance Requirements: SAT: 1310–1540   ACT: 28–32 HS GPA:

Degreed Writing Programs: English/Creative Writing

Sample Class Titles: Writing Argument • Writing Law • Travel Writing • Writing Description • Writing Creative Nonfiction • Screenwriting • Poetry and Being • Fiction Writing • Performance Poetry • Research for Writers • Writing Biography • Writing Profiles • Academic and Professional Writing • Television Writing • Playwriting • Writing the Graphic Novel

Instructor/Student Ratio: **Average Class Size**: 20
  1600 FT + 260 PT / 4,215 (1:2)

Success Stories

%of Students Who Go on to Graduate Study: 34%
Notable Writers From Faculty/Alumni:
Skrinath Reddy (poet) • Mark Strand (poet) • Richard Stern (novelist) • Susan Fromberg Schaeffer • Saul Bellow • Elizabeth Alexander • Campbell McGrath • David Auburn

Contact Information

Theodore O'Neill, Dean of Admissions
University of Chicago
1116 East 59th Street, Chicago, IL 60637
(773) 702 8650
http://www.uchicago.edu

University of Illinois—Chicago

Specifics

Entrance Requirements: SAT: ACT: 20–25 HS GPA:

Degreed Writing Programs: Communication • English

Sample Class Titles: Writing for the Electronic Media • Writing Nonfiction Prose • Writing for the Media • Writing Poetry • Writing Fiction • Literary Criticism • Teaching Writing • Novel Workshop

Instructor/Student Ratio: **Average Class Size**: 40
  1233 FT + 275 PT / 16,473

Success Stories

%of Students Who Go on to Graduate Study:
Notable Writers From Faculty/Alumni:
James McManus • Daniel Blackman • Michael Collins • Alex Shakar • Phyllis Moore • Cris Mozza • Luis Alberto Urrea • Ralph Mills • Lore Segal • James Park Sloan

Contact Information

Carol Snow, Executive Director of Admissions
University of Illinois—Chicago
PO Box 5220, Chicago, IL 60680
(312) 996 4350
uicadmit@uic.edu
http://www.uic.edu

Wheaton College

Specifics

Entrance Requirements: SAT: 1230–1420   ACT: 26–31 HS GPA: 3.0

Degreed Writing Programs: English/Writing

Sample Class Titles: Writing Effective Prose • Creative Writing • Advanced Writing • Poetry Writing and Criticism • Fiction Writing and Criticism • Composition • Writing Projects

Instructor/Student Ratio: **Average Class Size**: 30
183 FT + 104 PT / 2,353 (1:8)

Success Stories

%of Students Who Go on to Graduate Study:
Notable Writers From Faculty/Alumni:

Contact Information

Shawn Leftwich, Director of Admissions
Wheaton College
501 College Avenue, Wheaton, IL 60187
(630) 752 5005
admissions@wheaton.edu
http://www.wheaton.edu

A Final Word: Copyrights

Copyright is legal protection that ensures your ownership of your original work. Copyright in the United States was first mentioned in the Constitution. Therefore, it is a federally protected right.

According to the Copyright Office:

Copyright is a form of protection provided by the laws of the United States to the authors of "original works of authorship," including literary, dramatic, musical, artistic, and certain other intellectual works. This protection is available to both published and unpublished works. The 1976 Copyright Act generally gives the owner of copyright the exclusive right to do and to authorize others to do the following:

- *To reproduce the work in copies or phonorecords;*

- *To prepare derivative works based upon the work;*

- *To distribute copies or phonorecords of the work to the public by sale or other transfer of ownership, or by rental, lease, or lending;*

- *To perform the work publicly, in the case of literary, musical, dramatic, and choreographic works, pantomimes, and motion pictures and other audiovisual works;*

- *To display the work publicly, in the case of literary, musical, dramatic, and choreographic works, pantomimes, and pictorial, graphic, or sculptural works, including the individual images of a motion picture or other audiovisual work; and*

- *In the case of sound recordings*, *to perform the work publicly by means of a digital audio transmission.*

Copyright protection subsists from the time the work is created in fixed form. The copyright in the work of authorship immediately becomes the property of the author who created the work. Only the author or those deriving their rights through the author can rightfully claim copyright.

What this really means is that once you put your ideas down on paper, web, tape, or video, they belong to you. They are yours to keep or to sell, as you wish. You are the assumed owner of the material.

The reason many writers "file a copyright" with the Copyright Office is due to monetary protection.

For instance, when you have a book published, the publisher will file a copyright for the finished product in your name. However, magazines copyright their issues in their names. If you remember from an earlier section, you signed over your rights in order to get published.

The problem comes in with misuse. For instance, if the magazine takes your article and uses it in a book anthology that you have not signed rights to, that's misuse. Or if another magazine or website "borrows" your article for their readers, that's misuse. In these cases, if you have filed a copyright form with the Copyright Office, you don't have to prove you're the owner, the copyright form is all the proof you need to recover monetary damages from the perpetrator.

If you are being paid thousands of dollars for your material, filing a copyright is very important. If you're being paid $50 for a short article, the $45 copyright filing fee is probably not worth it.

As a professional writer, it's something you should know.

The U.S. Copyright Office is part of the Library of Congress. More information on copyrights can be found at http://www.copyright.gov/.

ChicagoWriter.com

For and about the business of writing.

Here's some of what you'll find on ChicagoWriter.com:

Word Wrangles ● Superior Vocabulary Builders

ChicagoWriter Date Book ● Write Education

Clients in Focus ● Webliography ● Legal Briefs

Job Links ● Salary Wizard ● Career Services

eBooks ● freeBooks ● Publishing News

We help writers succeed.

Chicago Writer **Books**

Name: _____

Address: _____

City: _____ State: _____ ZIP: _____

Telephone: _____

Email Address: _____

Payment: ☐ Check or Money Order ☐ VISA ☐ MasterCard

Card Number: _____ Exp Date: ___ /

Name: _____ Signature: _____

Billing Address (if different from shipping address): _____

City: _____ State: _____ ZIP: _____

# Copies	Title	Price Each	Total
	A Guide for Chicago's Young Writers (ISBN 978-1-933048-39-0)	$18.00	
	A Guide to Writing Jobs in Chicago, 3e (ISBN 978-1-933048-35-2)	$18.00	
	A Guide to Chicago's Zine Scene & Alternative Press (ISBN 978-1-933048-33-8)	$18.00	
	Please add 8.75% sales tax for all orders shipped to IL addresses.	Sales Tax	
	Shipping is free for orders over $50. For orders under $50, please add $5.95 shipping.	Shipping	
	TOTAL DUE		

All orders must be prepaid. Please remit order request along with credit card, check, or money order in $US to:

iWrite Publications Inc.
PO Box 10923
Chicago, IL 60610-0923